CASALS

Produced by Jonathan Wrice Schults, PHOTO EDITORS, INC.
Designed by Carmen Cavazos, Craven and Evans/Creative Graphics
Consultant, Sally Wecksler

Permission to use quotes from **Joys and Sorrows** by Pablo Casals,
as told to Albert E. Kahn, published by Simon and Schuster, has been graciously
given by Albert E. Kahn.

Translation for the English version of Casals' tribute to his mother
by Alfredo Matilla.

The wedding picture of Pablo and Marta Casals by Horace Gill.

Permission to use the music of ''Tres Estrofas de Amor'' granted by
Alexander Broude, Inc., 225 West 57th Street, New York, N.Y.   All rights reserved.

Published in Garden City, New York, by American Photographic Book Publishing
Co., Inc. All rights reserved. No part of this book may be reproduced in any form
without the written consent of the publisher.

Library of Congress Catalog Card No. 75-13882
ISBN: 0-8174-0593-3

Manufactured in the United States of America

INTRODUCTION

Finding Don Pablo's house in the multitude of barrios in San Juan, Puerto Rico was quite a feat. I remembered all the key words— Rio Piedras, Monterrey, Calle Himalaya. The first time, I found the house by sheer magic. It was high on a hill, surrounded by beautiful old laurel fig trees, quiet and away from the city noises.

The main door was wide open. Sounds of the cello came through faintly. It was the hour of the morning when the maestro practiced.

I entered, expecting to see a servant. The music became stronger. I followed it as if drawn by a magnet. The far end of the hall opened upon a large room where the small man sat playing. There are moments of ecstasy in my work and this was one of them. I was overcome by a feeling of shyness. But the maestro was in deep concentration. No other world existed except the music of Bach. My shyness was overcome by the compulsion to record this moment with the camera. Hardly moving from the spot, I worked fast and quietly. My presence was never noted; he made no sign. After he had finished the *sarabande,* he looked up and offered his hand. The hand was beautifully shaped, almost to the point of being delicate, but with a surprisingly strong grip.

"Nina, Nina, the photographer is here!"

His wife, Marta, came out of her little office just off the music room. She was young and beautiful.

Every day Don Pablo played from 10 to 11. It was only 10:30. He invited me to continue my work and not to mind his own complete concentration as he started to play again. It was then, that very first time, I made the photograph that pleased him so much. Weeks later, when he first saw it, he took the large print, went to his cello and played the same music again. Then, on the photograph, he wrote down the music he had been playing at the camera's click and signed it. He called it "Concentration."

In the Spring of 1973 we all sat on the veranda from where he could see over the green hills. Here, with friends, many of his famous observations were first spoken. As we sat listening, my camera was focused on his face following the moods of his conversation.

There was anger in his eyes when he spoke of the horror and futility of war, but when he marveled at the wonder of a seemingly insignificant plant, there was a happy expression on his face. Affectionately, he contemplated the huge trees which shaded his home, comparing their leaves to humanity.

Whenever I went to see the maestro and his wife, it was with great anticipation. I realized that I was trying to write with my camera and this might be the most difficult task of my career. A camera can sometimes estrange people, or it can bring them together. To the three of us, it became an instrument of friendship and pleasure.

In the afternoons, he would walk along the shady avenue leaning on his wife's arm. The hour of their walk was a happy time for them, as important as the morning hour of music.

There were days when Marta played audience and critic, even assisting him to correct a faulty position of the bridge on the cello. The house was run exactly to her planning, which was based on the complete understanding of her husband's wishes and needs. They were deeply in love and needed one another. It was beautiful to see them together. There was instant response, perfect harmony. Sadly, I realized that it could not last forever.

The last time we met, my wife Marguerite was with me and we both sensed that Don Pablo was in a heavy mood. With his eyes closed, his beloved pipe in his mouth, he talked of the previous night when he had felt that his soul had left his body. He said that he was soon to leave this world. He told us that there was no fear in him and that his life had been richly blessed with much beauty but whenever there had been periods of sadness, he had overcome them with his music. He spoke of his continued faith that man will overcome his drive toward destruction.

In the long life of Pablo Casals there was a driving force to make men understand each other. He was truly a free soul. Freedom meant everything to him.

This visit seemed to close the circle. As I left, it was not only the harmony of the music but the harmony of life that flooded my being.

Fritz Henle

HOW THESE PICTURES WERE TAKEN

Those to whom the camera is an instrument of artistic expression know the seemingly endless possibilities that photography makes available to the creative mind.

There are, of course, no secrets; new techniques soon become common knowledge. Hence, while mastery of one's equipment is essential, the photographer's real challenge rests with his ability to understand his subject matter.

Of the many versatile camera systems available, I use one almost exclusively—the Rolleiflex SL66. I have used it ever since its development and all of my photographs of Pablo and Marta Casals were taken with it. This is an intimate camera; the fact that I do not have to hold it close to my eyes when taking pictures makes it a part of me. While talking with my subject, whole conversations can be captured with but a few glances into the ground glass. And this is where life actually happens for me—on my ground glass. There I am instantly aware of the split second in which to release the shutter.

From the beginning, I was fascinated by the atmosphere Marta and Pablo Casals had created in their lovely home on Calle Himalaya, high above San Juan. Fortunately, too, it was usually flooded with light, which solved the difficult problem of Don Pablo's extreme sensitivity to the brilliant flash of strobe light. All of the photographs were taken in available light, using the Kodak Tri-X Pan film that I favor. Reading this film at an ASA speed of 200 (well below its advertised ASA 400) permitted the relatively short development time that produced almost no grain in the images.

To be allowed to photograph Don Pablo, in his own home and without any restrictions, was one of the great privileges of my life. The most productive times were the early morning hours when he seemed to live in another world—his mind was with his music. Then I could move around freely, changing lenses as I saw fit and without any embarrassment that I might disturb him. The close-ups were all created with the 150mm lens; the longshot, where he is playing his cello in front of his piano, was done with an 80mm lens. Then, without changing my position, I also captured him with the 150 and 200mm lenses. Of course, I had my SL66 on a tripod.

The studies of his expressions were done on the terrace, with the camera on a tripod so low that I used a sitting position to compose my pictures on the ground glass and make the few simple adjustments that were needed. When friends joined us and Don Pablo spoke with them, I could follow his expressions in the ground glass. I was part of the group and so was my camera. Most of these exposures were done at a relatively fast speed—1/125th and even 1/250th of a second. The diffused light on the terrace was bright enough to permit f/stops from 8–11. This was all I needed.

It was different, of course, when I worked with him inside. On bright days, I could use 1/60th of a second with an f/stop of 8, but many times I had to rely on a slower speed. This can be done when one is extremely careful to follow the movements of the musician and anticipate the peaks of the phrases in a composition.

At times, very fast changes were necessary. My usual practice of carrying four cassettes provided me with 48 exposures. Since I have a high degree of control, this gave me many possibilities. While cassettes also make it possible to quickly change from black and white to color film, I did not take advantage of this opportunity since I felt the black and white medium was more suitable for most of the Casals' collection.

In the candid pictures, such as those of the daily walks with Marta, and some of their close-ups, the camera was hand held. For these pictures, I had to be absolutely free to change the camera position within a split second. Here I could rely on the firm grip of my hand and my ability to hold the camera absolutely still. This is a matter of long training, but it can be crucial, especially when it comes to poor light with relatively long exposures. On the walks, especially, a tripod would have been a great hindrance—physically as well as psychologically—although in this case Marta and Pablo Casals accepted me completely.

It is this acceptance for which a photographer must constantly strive and train. Once it is achieved, and the camera becomes second nature, the camera system used no longer plays the all-important role. Be it 35mm, my favorite SL66, or any other camera—if you understand the drama of life, its beauty, ugliness and poetry, then you hold in your hands the perfect instrument to parallel your own vision.

BIOGRAPHICAL NOTES

When I met Pablo Casals in 1972 he was 95 years old. His spirit was young and he was still the vital force of the Festival Casals, the yearly musical event in San Juan, Puerto Rico.

The maestro had strong ties to the island through his mother who was born in Mayaguez, P.R., of Catalan parents. Casals' mother returned to Spain when she was eighteen and Don Pablo was born in Vendrell near Barcelona on December 29, 1876.

His father, the church organist, was a fine musician and teacher. He taught the young Pau to play the piano and violin before he was seven years old. Soon the young boy learned to write music and developed an interest in the cello.

Casals began his formal studies at the age of eleven at the Municipal School of Music in Barcelona. He graduated in 1891 and, continuing to progress rapidly, he attracted the attention of the wealthy Count de Morphy who became his patron and introduced him to the royal court at Madrid, where he played regularly for Queen Christina.

Casals' mother, at great sacrifice, devoted her life to his development as a musician and a man. His debut, November 12, 1899, as soloist in Lalo's cello concerto conducted by Lamoureux in Paris, was a great success. His career launched, he gave concerts in Europe's capital cities, South America and the United States. The violinist Jacques Thibaud and the pianist Alfred Cortot joined Casals to form the famous trio. After World War I, Casals, always fascinated by the orchestra, founded his own in Barcelona and became guest conductor of many great orchestras including the New York and London symphonies.

In 1936, when civil war broke out in Spain, Casals supported the Loyalist Government, which was defeated. He settled in Prades, a small town near the Spanish border in the French Pyrenees. He stayed in France during World War II, offering encouragement and support to his fellow exiles. After the war, Casals became convinced that he could not end his exile and continued to live in Prades. Musicians, pupils and friends from all over the world flocked to him.

In 1950, with the inspiration of his friend Alexander Schneider, the violinist, he laid the foundation for the Prades Festival.

In 1957, he married Marta Montanez, an advanced cello student from Puerto Rico. By coincidence, Marta's mother had the same birthdate as Casals' mother and was born in the same house in Mayaguez. Photographs showed that Marta bore a striking resemblance to Casals' mother, Pilar.

Again, the vision of Alexander Schneider played a role in Casals' making his home in Puerto Rico and forming the Festival there. He was the focal point for the great musicians who convened there. The couple traveled to the mainland often—a recital at the United Nations in 1958, the White House to play for President Kennedy in 1961, summers at the Marlboro Music Festival in Vermont for the Masters Classes that are still televised throughout the world.

In 1973, the famous couple traveled to Mexico and to Israel. One of Casals' last messages was to encourage the people of Israel.

It was an inspiration to see him, at 96 years of age, conduct the famous musicians he had worked with over the years. His strong gestures and expressions generated excitement. One could actually hear him sing.

An artistic performance
is the blending of
intelligence and
intuition. We must
look for the meaning
of music and this is
only to be found
when the performer
approaches it with
honesty and humility.

There is, of course, no substitute for work. I myself practice constantly, as I have all my life. I have been told I play the cello with the ease of a bird flying. I do not know with how much effort a bird learns to fly, but I do know what effort has gone into my cello. What seems ease of performance comes from the greatest labor.

I have never drawn an artificial line between teaching and learning. A teacher, of course, should know more than his pupil. But for me, to teach is to learn.

Each day I am reborn. All my life I have started each day in
the same manner. It is not a mechanical routine, but something
essential to my daily life. First I go to nature; it is a rediscovery
of the world of which I have the joy of being a part. It fills me
with the awareness of the wonder of life, with a feeling of
incredible marvel of being a human being. Then, I go to
the piano and I play two Preludes and Fugues of Bach.
It is a sort of benediction on the house. The music is never
the same for me, each day is something new, fantastic
and unbelievable. That is Bach, like nature, a miracle.

Life has become too complicated, we should look at the beautiful and simple things of nature and of life. We should never underestimate life nor lose touch with it, by respecting and loving life in every sense— one's own and that of others— and resisting the temptation of going against moral and spiritual values.

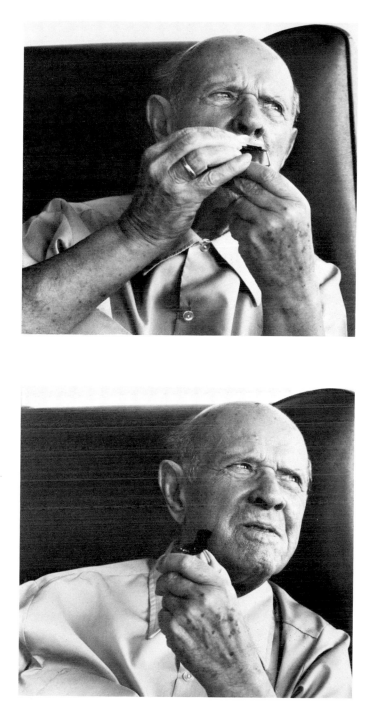

. . . each musician must learn
to play, on the one hand, as if
he were a soloist and, on the
other, with the constant
awareness of being an
indispensable part of a team.
It is this quality of human
teamwork . . . that has always
afforded me a joy as a
conductor that no solo
performance can duplicate.

Of all the pupils I have taught, Martita was one of the best. I was impressed from the onset not only by her musical talent but by her remarkable aptitude. I have never had a pupil who learned more rapidly or worked with greater discipline. At the same time, though studying an instrument is, of course, a serious affair, she brought an irrepressible brightness of spirit to her work. Her gaiety was infectious.

I shared in his moments of joy and fulfillment, daily concerns and problems, and in his profound thoughts about the suffering of the world and the way in which we, as individuals, could help alleviate it.

Marta Casals

He left us so much and especially to me. In every way: in terms of his music, his humanism, his philosophy, his example. All this remains with me. I feel a great loss and sorrow but, in a way, he prepared me very well for this moment, and I am sure he would be disappointed if I were to discontinue my involvement with life because of my suffering. But one must overcome it by doing positive things. This is what he always did, and what I am trying to do.

Music must serve a purpose; it must be a part of something larger than itself, a part of humanity, and that, indeed, is at the core of my argument with music of today—its lack of humanity. A musician is also a man, and more important than his music is his attitude toward life. Nor can the two be separated.

We live in an age in which we have accomplished magnificent things and made miraculous advances, an age in which man embarks upon the exploration of the stars. Yet on our planet we continue to act like barbarians. Like barbarians, we fear our neighbors on the earth; we arm against them and they arm against us. The time has come when this must be halted if man is to survive. We must become accustomed to the fact that we are human beings.

I have observed a curious trait in many men—
though they do not hesitate to say how much they
love their mothers, they are reticent to say how
much they love their wives!

Casals' Mother

Marta and Pablo's Wedding

There is no such reticence in me. Martita is the
marvel of my world, and each day I find some new
wonder in her. I am aware that I am no longer
exactly a youth, but if I speak of her in words perhaps
expected of young lovers, it is because that is how
I feel about her. Perhaps, indeed, because I have
lived longer than most people, I have learned
more than most about the meaning of love . . . .

Una madre por naturaleza es una cosa sublime, pero a mi madre hay que ponerla en un plano aparte. No es lo mismo ser una buena madre que una madre excepcional por el carácter y personalidad propia. Yo no he conocido a ninguna mujer — y he conocido muchas madres en mi vida — como ella. Cada palabra que ella decía tenía un sentido profundo, por su inteligencia, por su intuición, por naturaleza.

Sabía de todo; de música, de medicina, de arquitectura, de agricultura, — no solamente porque había estudiado, sino, y sobretodo porque comprendía. Quizás lo más admirable era su altísimo fundamento moral. Vivía mucho más avanzada que su época, además era tan noble y tan hermosa. Personas superiores que la trataron veían en ella una personalidad extraordinaria.

Mi madre fué una mujer genial.

Pablo Casals

A mother, by nature, is something sublime, but my mother must be placed on a different plane. To be a good mother is not the same as being an exceptional mother because of character and distinct personality. I do not know of any other woman like her – and I have known many mothers all through my life. Each word she uttered made profound sense, because of her intelligence, her intuition, her nature.

She knew about everything: music, medicine, architecture, agriculture – not only because she studied, but also because, above everything, she understood. Maybe what was most admirable about her was her high moral standard. She lived ahead of her time; and moreover, she was so noble and so beautiful. Superior persons who came in contact with her saw in her an extraordinary personality.

My mother was a genius.

Pablo Casals

There are, I know, people who do not love animals, but I think this is because they do not understand them—or because, indeed, they do not really see them. For me, animals have always been a special part of the wonder of nature—the smallest as well as the largest—with their amazing variety, their beautifully contrived shapes and fascinating habits. I am captivated by the spirit of them. I find in them a longing to communicate and a real capacity for love. If sometimes they do not trust but fear man, it is because he has treated them with arrogance and insensitivity.

. . . I am a man first, an artist second. As a man, my first obligation is to the welfare of my fellow men. I will endeavor to meet this obligation through music—the means which God has given me—since it transcends language, politics and national boundaries. My contribution to world peace may be small, but at least I will have given all I can to an ideal I hold sacred.

Sometimes I look about me with a feeling of complete dismay. In the confusion that afflicts the world today, I see a disrespect for the very values of life. Beauty is all about us, but how many are blind to it! They look at the wonder of this earth and seem to see nothing. People move hectically but give little thought to where they are going. They seek excitement for its mere sake, as if they were lost and desperate.

An affront to human dignity
is an affront to me, and
to protest injustice is
a matter of conscience.
Are human rights of less
importance to an artist
than to other men? Does
being an artist exempt
one from his obligations
as a man? If anything,
the artist has a particular

responsibility, because he has been granted special sensitivities and perceptions, and because his voice may be heard when others are not. Who, indeed, should be more concerned than the artist with the defense of liberty and free inquiry, which are essential to his very creativity?

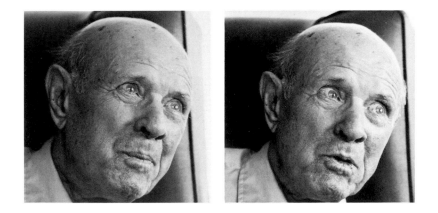

Music, that wonderful
universal language, should
be a source of communication
among men. I once again
exhort my fellow musicians
throughout the world to put
the purity of their art at the
service of mankind in order to
unite all people in fraternal
ties. Let each of us contribute
as he is able until this ideal is
attained in all its glory.

I was born with an ability, with music in me, that is all. No special credit was due me. The only credit we claim is for the use we make of the talent we are given. That is why I urge young musicians:Don't be vain because you happen to have talent. You are not responsible for that; it was not of your doing. What you do with your talent is what matters. You must cherish this gift. Do not demean or waste what you have been given. Work—work constantly and nourish it.

My cello is my
oldest friend,
my dearest friend.

Either you believe in what you are doing or you do not. Music is something to be approached with integrity, not something to be turned on or off like tap water.

Work helps prevent one
from getting old. I, for
one, cannot dream of retiring.
Not now or ever. Retire?
The word is alien and the
idea inconceivable to me.
I don't believe in retirement
for anyone in my type of
work, not while the spirit
remains. My work is my

life. I cannot think of one
without the other. To
retire means to begin to
die. The man who works and
is never bored is never
old. Work and interest
are the best remedy for
age. Each day I am
reborn. Each day I
must begin again.

I have always regarded technique as a means, not an end in itself. One must, of course, master technique; at the same time, one must not become enslaved by it. One must understand that the purpose of technique is to transmit the inner meaning, the message, of the music.

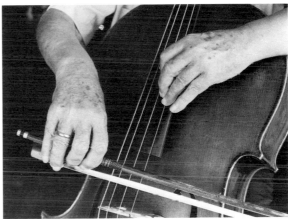

The most perfect technique is that which is not noticed at all.

Intuition is the decisive element in both the composing and the performance of music. Of course technique and intelligence have vital functions—one must master the technique of an instrument in order to extract its full potentialities and one must apply one's intelligence in exploring every facet of the music—but ultimately, the paramount role is that of intuition. For me the determining factor in creativity, in bringing a work to life, is that of musical instinct.

Monotony is the worst enemy of music.

You ask what my legacy to the world is. It is always the same—the lesson of never underestimating life, of never losing touch with it. To respect and love life in every sense, one's own and that of others. To resist doing things that have no meaning for life.

Duration about 5 mins.

Dedicated to Marta Casals

Tres Estrofas de Amor

Three Verses of Love
for Soprano and Piano

Tomas Blanco
English version by
Marta Casals and Doris Madden

Pablo Casals
(1958)

Mi-ra en las o-las del mar co-mo te
See in the waves of the sea How much I

quie-ro:— Te quie-ro por las hon-du-ras de mis des-
love you. I love you from the depths of my

ve - los.
sleep - less-ness,

Que a - mor, que a-
For love is the

mor es el tras-fon - do de re-
in - ner mem - o - ry of far - a-

mo - tos a - ye - res.
way times, of yes - ter-days.

Agitato come prima

A. B. 152-7

Mi-ra_en la no - che se -
See in the peace - ful

Tempo II

cresc. e accel. poco a poco

re - na co - mo te quie - ro: ____ Te
night How much I love you. ____ I

cresc. e accel. poco a poco

quie - ro por las al - tu - ras de mis en - sue - ños. Que a -
love you from ____ the heights ____ of my dreams, For

mor es__ la pro - me - sa del e-ter-no ma - ña - na.
love___ is the prom-ise of e-ter-nal to - mor - rows.

Mi-ra en la ca - ña flo -
See in the blos - som-ing

ri - da co - mo te quie - ro:__ Te quie - ro por las lla -
flow - er How much I love you. I love you from__ the

nu - ras de mi so sie - go Te quie - ro por las lla - nu - ras de mi so-sie - go.
calm of my con-tent-ment, I love you from the calm of my con-tent - ment,

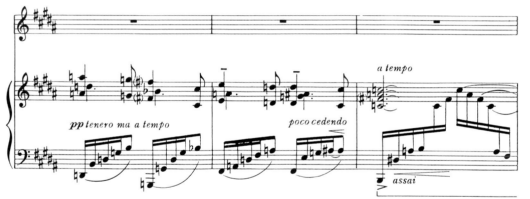

a tempo

pp tenero ma a tempo   *poco cedendo*

assai

poco rit. p   a tempo

Que a - mor es el per - fu - me del mi-la-gro pre -
For love is like a fra-grance en-hanc-ing the

cunt.

poco rit.

a tempo

A. B. 152-7

sen - te. Te quie - ro en ul - tra - ma - res de es-
spring air. I love you, I love you be-

pa - cio y tiem - po; Te quie - ro a flor de
yond space and time; I love you on this

tie - rra ya - ho - ra te quie - ro, Te quie - ro, Te
earth, and now, I love you, I love you, I

quie - - ro.
love   you.

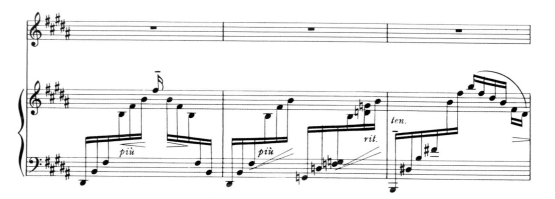

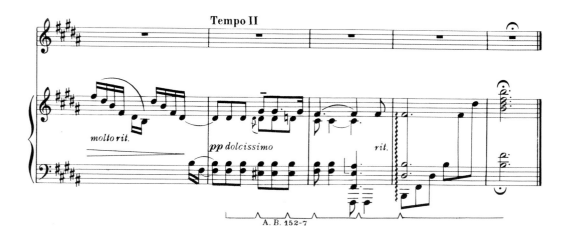

One's work should be a salute to life.

I am perhaps the oldest musician
in the world. I am an old man, but
in many senses I am a very young
man. And this is what I want you to
be—young, young all your life,
and to say things to the world
that are true. Goodness, love—
this is the real world. Let us have
love, love and peace.

(Speech at Central Park, N.Y.,
June 1973)

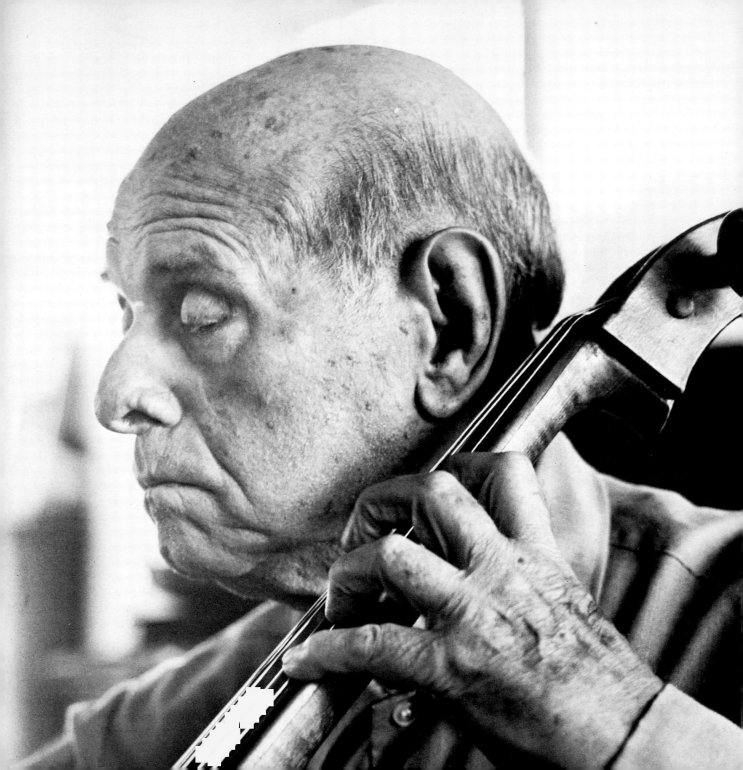

Fritz Henle has asked me to write some words about his book. I believe I need make no comment on his photographs. They speak for themselves, and the reader, I know, will understand if I do not write about the subject with which they largely deal. My life with my husband is a matter of personal intimacy. There are many everlasting, beautiful memories and I feel privileged to have shared his unique and fulfilled life. He was and always will be an immeasurably precious part of my existence.

There are endless tributes to Pablo Casals and it is impossible for me to express within a few lines the full nature of the emotions I feel on looking back at our life together. I will only point out some essential traits as a human being that were present in every detail of his everyday life.

As a man, he was seemingly small, and yet he was a giant in beauty and spirit. Though tender and apparently fragile, delicately tuned to every whisper of sound and thread of loveliness, he had within him an indomitable strength. Those who knew him closely felt the special qualities of his personality—his warmth, his optimism, his understanding, his boundless humanity. He had a radiance and magnetism that affected all around him.

All of his life, during which he brought such joy and beauty to the world, he fought against dark forces in it, no matter what the odds. He never wavered in his love of mankind and his struggle to end human suffering and oppression. He opposed war and waged his own unceasing one against it. A noble warrior of greatly gentle heart, he fought for the life of man until the last and never lost his faith in mankind.

His spirit, his message will live on. As his music will never be forgotten, so what he stood for as a man will always be remembered.

Marta Casals

San Juan, Puerto Rico
January, 1974